THE DEAD SEA SCROLLS

Sarah Blackmore

Published in association with The Basic Skills Agency

Hodder & Stoughton

A MEMBER OF THE HODDER HEADLINE

Acknowledgements

Cover: Darren Lock

Illustrations: Maureen Carter

Photos: Popperfoto/Reuters

Every effort has been made to trace copyright holders of material reproduced in this book. Any rights not acknowledged will be acknowledged in subsequent printings if notice is given to the publisher.

Orders; please contact Bookpoint Ltd, 39 Milton Park, Abingdon, Oxon OX14 4TD. Telephone: (44) 01235 400414, Fax: (44) 01235 400454. Lines are open from 9.00–6.00, Monday to Saturday, with a 24 hour message answering service.
Email address: orders@bookpoint.co.uk

British Library Cataloguing in Publication Data
A catalogue record for this title is available from the British Library

ISBN 0 340 77649 8

First published 2000
Impression number   10 9 8 7 6 5 4 3 2 1
Year   2005 2004 2003 2002 2001 2000

Copyright © 1999 NTC/Contemporary Publishing Group, Inc.

Adapted for the Livewire series by Sarah Blackmore

Typeset by GreenGate Publishing Services, Tonbridge, Kent.
Printed in Great Britain for Hodder and Stoughton Educational, a division of Hodder Headline Plc, 338 Euston Road, London NW1 3BH, by Redwood Books, Trowbridge, Wilts

Contents

This is a story of hidden treasure.
Real treasure that lay hidden
for over 1,000 years.
Think about it.

You may have heard about time capsules.
All sorts of things are put into them.
Things that show what our life is like now.
Time capsules are buried in the ground.
It is hoped that people in the future
will find them.

What would you put in a time capsule?
It would need to tell people in the future
about your life now.

Now, think about finding a time capsule almost 2,000 years after it was buried. Would you know what it was?

What if you found it by accident? Who would you tell? What would you do with it?

This is what happened to a young boy in 1947.

1 The Goat-herd

A young boy worked as a goat-herd.
He looked after his family's goats.
Every day he took the goats out to feed.
It was his job to make sure
that they did not get lost.

The boy took the goats into the hills.
He lived near the Dead Sea.
The Dead Sea is in Jordan –
a country in the Middle East.

One day the boy noticed
that one of the goats was missing.
He went to look for it.
As he was looking he saw something.
It was a small hole in the rocks.
It was the opening to a cave.

2 A Secret Cave

The boy picked up a stone.
He tossed it into the cave.
The stone should have hit
the wall of the cave.
The boy waited to hear the echo.
Instead he heard a different sound.

He heard the sound of something breaking.
What could it be?

The boy did not know what the sound was.
He was frightened.
He ran away.

He told his friend what had happened.
They went back to the cave together.
They thought there might be
some hidden treasure.

The two boys squeezed through the hole
in the rocks.
They dropped into the cave.
They looked around for treasure.

The boys hoped that they would see gold.
They hoped that they would see
treasure chests.
What did they see?

There was no gold.
Only some old clay jars.

3 The Scrolls

The boys looked at the clay jars.
They opened the lid on one.
They looked inside.

They saw something folded up.
It looked like pieces of cloth.

The boys pulled the cloth out of the jars.
There was something wrapped in the cloth.
They opened it up.
Inside were some pieces of leather.
They had writing on them.
They were scrolls.

Some of the scrolls were about 1 metre long.
Some were about 8 metres long.
The writing was strange.
The boys could not understand it.
It looked very old.

The boys took all the scrolls
that they could find.
They could have thrown them away –
but they took them to sell.

4 Real or False?

At first the boys tried to sell the scrolls
in Bethlehem.
They showed them to a man.
He liked to buy old things.
The man was not interested.
He did not think that the scrolls
were important.

The boys tried to sell them to other people.
At last somebody bought them.
They did not pay the boys very much.

Some of the scrolls were later sold
to the Hebrew University.
Some were sold to a man called Samuel.
He was a monk.

Lots of people looked at the scrolls.
Many of them were experts.
They tried to work out what the scrolls were.

Some thought that they were not
worth anything.
One expert thought that the scrolls
were fakes.
Other experts could not believe
their good luck.
They could tell that the scrolls were real.
They could tell that the scrolls
were a great discovery.
One of the greatest discoveries
of modern times.

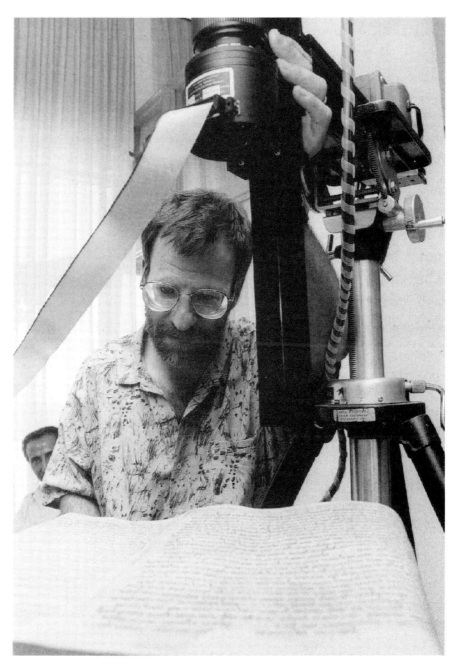

Professor Bearman photographs part of the Dead Sea Scrolls.

The experts said that the scrolls
were very old.
They thought they might be
more than 2,000 years old.
A special test was used to work out
just how old the scrolls were.
It is called a carbon test.
This test showed that the scrolls had been written
between 200 BC and AD 68.

The scrolls were called the Dead Sea Scrolls.
They turned out to be parts
of the Old Testament of the Bible.

5 More Caves

People who studied the Bible were excited.
The scrolls were the oldest parts of the Bible
to be found.

Lots of people went to look for more caves.
They hoped to find more scrolls –
and they did.

They found more caves and more scrolls.
By 1956 they had found ten more caves.

These are some of the things they found.

Cave 2
More parts of the Old Testament.

Cave 3
A scroll written on copper.
It was called the Copper Scroll.
This scroll was like a treasure map.
It showed where there was hidden treasure.
Treasures of gold and silver.

A fragment of Christian text.

Cave 4

This cave had been man-made.
Lots of things were found here.
There were parts from almost every book
in the Old Testament.
There were also books on war.
There were even books about the laws
of that time.

6 Why, What and Who

Why are the Dead Sea Scrolls so important?
Well for one thing some were written
at the time of Jesus.
Do you remember the time capsule?
The scrolls tell us about life 2,000 years ago.

What languages were the scrolls written in?
A lot of the scrolls were in Hebrew.
A few were written in Greek.
The exciting thing is …
some were written in the same language
that Jesus spoke.
This language is called Aramaic.

The Elizabeth Hay Bechtel Psalms Scroll before unrolling.

Who wrote the scrolls?
It is hard to say.
Most people think that it was a group
of Jews called the Essenes.
They lived near the Dead Sea.

Why did they hide the scrolls?
Nobody really knows.
It may have been to keep them safe
from Roman soldiers.
The caves were close by.
They made a good hiding place.

7 What a Find!

The scrolls gave people a chance
to check the Bible.
Before the scrolls were found the oldest
Bible had been translated from Greek.
Nobody was sure that the translation was right.

The scrolls did tell us some new things.
Some books in the Old Testament
had to be changed a bit.

However, the basic beliefs of Jews and Christians
did not change.
The scrolls agreed with most
of the Greek translation.

The Dead Sea Scrolls have helped us
to find out more about our world.
They have told us more about the people
who lived 2,000 years ago
and about what life was like
all those years ago.

What a time capsule.
What a treasure!